BABY, YOUR GIFT WILL MAKE ROOM FOR YOU.

How my knack for cultivating critical connections transformed my life, business, and career.

MONIQUE LARUE

BABY, YOUR GIFT WILL MAKE ROOM FOR YOU.

1. Networking 2. Mindset 3. Change (Psychology)

Printed in the United States of America.

For information address monique@moniquelaurue.com | Monique LaRue Consulting & Media LLC.
227 Sandy Springs PL, Suite D437, Atlanta GA 30328

Book cover and layout by Michelle Samplin-Salgado

ISBN: 978-1-7357549-0-1

DEDICATION

For my mother, Sonia Mercedes Holst, my most meaningful connection, for her total belief that my gift would make room for me. To Spirit who continues to guide and lead me on my journey to and through critical connections.

TABLE OF CONTENTS

FOREWORD

When I first received an email from Monique, I could tell that she was excited about something. Her enthusiasm shined through the words that almost jumped off the screen. Later when we met for lunch, she excitedly shared more about her cultivating critical connections concept (the Mindful Connector Method™). When I listened to her talk and then later read the notes for her book, I knew she was onto something big. Her passion for the project was contagious, and I immediately wanted to help her with this endeavor.

Monique truly understands servant leadership and embodies the characteristics of a Level 5 leader. In Jim Collins' book, *Good to Great*, Collins describes the Level 5 leader as "...one who operates first with genuine humility, humility defined as a burning, passionate, obsessive ambition for the cause or work and not themselves and a will to make good on those ambitions."

Monique values relationships and knows that you get more out of life when you help others. When she states that she wrote the book for you, the future leaders of our world, she means it. She wants you to have a jumpstart on the important life-changing lessons. She wants you to learn early the art of personal and professional expansion.

As you read this book, you will quickly see why it is important to connect with others and to build lifelong relationships. If you want to be a leader, you must realize that it is all about people. Her Mindful Connector Method™ framework gives you a method for connecting deeply with people, while at the same time helping them become the best that they can be.

As I read this book, I could not help but remember that wonderful movie, *Pay It Forward*. When we are serving others, we are making this world a better place.

In this book, you will find a quick reference guide to help you remember the technique for cultivating critical connections. Monique will ask you first to look inward at your own strengths, vulnerabilities, beliefs, and values. Only when you look inward can you look outward.

You must first understand yourself before you can build relationships with others. Monique will ask you to start by knowing where you are going so that you can connect with the right people. I can hear her saying it now: "You have got to understand where you want to be personally and professionally."

~ *Deborah Roebuck, Ph.D., Atlanta, Georgia*

INTRODUCTION

Hi there! If you have picked up this book, then you probably already have some sense of the importance of connecting with others both in the workplace and in your life. I am lucky enough to have been born with a natural ability to connect to others. I was outgoing from the start. As a child, my mother would watch me approach the adults around me and strike up conversations without any hesitation. She sometimes wondered if there might be something wrong with me because I had no fear.

I didn't have to give the skill of connecting with others a single thought. It worked for me every time I needed it to work. I attended an HBCU (Historically Black College and University); as you continue to read along, you'll understand why I'm highlighting that fact. Attending university was a great opportunity for me to explore many interests and to develop and grow as a person. In college, we (my classmates and I) were just going through the motions. Connecting or networking in a particular way for a profession wasn't something we were taught. Perhaps kids in other cultures were taught to build networks in college or early in life. I didn't have any of that knowledge firsthand and I'm sure many of my classmates were in the same boat.

I remember a time when I was asked to be the mistress of ceremonies for an event at the college. One of the campus staff members couldn't get the person they wanted. After the event, the staffer approached me and said, "You know Monique, I didn't know you could speak that well." I believe they may have been referring to the ebbs and flows of my delivery, the clarity of the pronunciation of the words I spoke. I was just reading off of the paper that was given to me. It was a bizarre comment, but one I had heard before. I didn't realize then how much having this natural ability to connect and to articulate in various ways would help shape the success (at least what I deemed success) of my professional life in the future. Bonding with supervisors in my work-study jobs, during internships, and summer work programs was easy. I wasn't quite sure why, but I felt different and I wouldn't really get a good grasp of that ability until much later in life.

It wasn't until I started thinking about what came after college that I really considered the importance of the way I communicated and was able to make trustworthy connections. From that line of thinking, I began considering the spirit of forming connections and how, despite my natural ability, it was both complex and multifaceted. Once I left the homogeneous community in which I had spent most of my life, I started asking myself why I was connecting; were those connections meaningful and critical to my life? Would I know who to form connections with? Would it be different as a black woman in the working world than it had been in other aspects of my life?

As these questions swirled, I came to my second realization. There were no structures in place to teach other students early on the significance of connections, especially in the HBCU community, how to recognize meaningful connections, and how to create them in the workplace and in life. There were no mentors, coaches, or classes geared toward the topic. We were simply expected to infer these skills, though I had them naturally.

So, I set about educating myself and others about the idea of establishing trustworthy relationships that were mutually beneficial and could foster lifelong growth and expansion for the people who were connecting. When I moved on to my master's degree at Kennesaw State University, I was invited to give a talk to underclassmen about the ideas I had begun developing on creating these vital connections. I hadn't yet termed it Cultivating Critical Connections, but the underlying principles are the same. From there I began broadening my talks on the subject to include other universities and companies that requested them.

Why I Wrote This Book

Each time I showed up for a talk, I was asked the same question: "Do you have a book?" At first, I couldn't even imagine sitting down to write a book, but the more I thought about it, the more I understood that people wanted something to take away. Today we are tech advanced and there are so many options, but in the beginning a book meant credibility.

This book is intended to teach an easily transferable three-step approach to creating vital relationships that help people win in business and in life. What I now call the Mindful Connector Method™ is the system that will help anyone, from college-bound students and young adults to professionals at the height of their careers. If I had the wisdom nuggets you're going to get in this book twenty years ago, the big playing field I have right now would be even more incredible.

What to Expect from This Book

This book was designed to be a hands-on guide to Cultivating Critical Connections.

Throughout this book you can expect to learn:

- The difference between simple networking and real, meaningful, worthwhile critical connections.
- How to differentiate between deep connections and superficial connections.
- How to determine who you should be connecting with.
- To gauge the interest and willingness of others to engage in a mutually beneficial connection.

- The techniques using the Mindful Connector Method™ to ensure that you are intentional about your approach to building these connections.

This book was not intended to be a passive reading experience. Instead, it was designed to encourage a dynamic intentional experience that allows you to immediately apply the advice and techniques directly to your daily experiences.

Get ready to dive right in, push the boundaries of your comfort zone, and start cultivating critical connections!

Chapter One

WHAT ARE CRITICAL CONNECTIONS?

You can make more friends in two months being interested in other people than in two years trying to get people interested in you.

– Dale Carnegie

I am pretty confident in the assumption that the majority of the people reading this book have heard the word "networking" more than once throughout their careers. Networking is the big buzzword since the early 2000s, coinciding with the boom of interconnectedness through cell phones, internet and emails. Since then, classes just for networking have cropped up in colleges and adult workshops everywhere.

Yet, networking as both a term and a concept is self-limiting. Networking refers to work relationships, which tend toward the superficial, focused on the primary goal of bettering our own position in work or life.

When you read articles about networking, you are inundated with the benefits of job offers, improving sales, and enhanced social standing. The accepted definition coined by Andrew Hennigan in his book *Payforward Networking* is, "Networking is a deliberate activity to build, reinforce and maintain relationships of trust with other people to further your goals."[1] Note that the definition includes the limited purpose of furthering only your own goals.

This definition and the renewed push for networking essentially created an unspoken expectation that professionals should be constantly on the lookout for opportunities to further their careers. I see this unhealthy mentality even now. When I started consulting, the first step I always had my clients complete was a self-check vision statement of why they wanted to improve their strategies for connecting. Time and again their reasons focused almost entirely on improving their career or getting something from the person and business they were connecting with. And don't we all want to get something back for our connections? But therein lies the first mistake. **No critical relationship relies on a foundation of selfish purposes.**

A recent study sheds further light on the negative side effects of modern networking as defined by industry leaders. The study called *The Contaminating Effects of Building Instrumental Ties: How Networking Can Make Us Feel Dirty*[2] details the damaging effects of networking based solely on reaching professional goals on our self-perceptions. In other words, when individuals in the study engaged in networking, they felt less positive about themselves.

If you haven't guessed by now, critical connections are so much more than simply networking. Critical connections are long term, mutually beneficial, trustworthy relationships, but even more than that, critical connections speak to the intention behind forming the relationship. On some level, we all form relationships to get something, whether it is companionship, friendship, job prospects, or promotions,

but the magic happens when you cultivate a critical connection with someone else.

If you find you are forming relationships only to get something back or move up the corporate ladder, you are networking, you are not forming critical connections, and that may be the very reason you are coming up against roadblocks and frustration.

Why are Critical Connections so Important?

At some point in our lives, we realize we are who we are because of the critical connections we've made. When we take the time to create genuine connections, we make it clear that we value the people we are connecting with.

The philosophy of the Mindful Connector Method™ is really simple: **If we take the time to master how we cultivate relationships, examine the fine details of what's critical (vital) in our relationships, and then commit to the effort of keeping those connections intact, we can change the trajectory of our lives as well as the lives of others.**

When I first started helping others develop critical connections, I was surprised by just how ill-equipped people from all walks of life are to form trustworthy, connected relationships. Some years ago, a group of five college students came into my life, a situation that spurred me to further develop the concept of cultivating critical connections. I worked for a nonprofit technology organization where I created, managed, and implemented a mentoring program for what were considered "disadvantaged" students from a local two-year technical college. The students ranged in age from twenty-four to forty, and without the program, they wouldn't have otherwise had the opportunity to connect with chief information officers from Fortune 500 companies.

The program required that I pair students with executive-level professionals at major corporations in the area. When I was a student, I would have considered this an ideal situation to take advantage of, given my natural ability to establish rapport and quickly find synergy with others. However, as I coached these students, I saw something very different from what I had expected happening between the students and the executives. Both parties in the pairing struggled to make a connection, and they failed to find the critical factors that would be beneficial to one another.

After completing the evaluation of that year-long program, I realized that the CIOs often took for granted the opportunities they had, so when thrown into this new experience, they didn't have the necessary skill set to lean on to form unique connections. Similarly, the students didn't have the foundational skills to foster connections with people so far removed from their own situation.

From this, I decided to develop a platform to prepare students and everyone else for this type of interaction. I understood that navigating the process of cultivating critical connections could be tricky since it involves many factors, including a wide variety of circumstances, situations, and personality types, but I also understood that **when a critical connection is made, it is more than a rewarding event. It can change lives.**

Without critical connections, on the other hand, many students and professionals will follow a linear, often predefined path that is constrained by traditional superficial networking. Learning relationship-building skills can have a serious impact, both personally and professionally. Students, adults, and professionals who haven't developed these skills will be challenged as they try to interact in the workplace.

What Makes a Strong Critical Connection?

At this point, you may be thinking about the relationships you have formed so far and wondering, "Does this fit into the definition of a critical connection?" And that is a good question. It is always important to be an active participant in your relationships and determine if your relationships are healthy, worthwhile, and strong. Strong is defined as 1) able to withstand great force or pressure and 2) firmly held or established. When thinking about your connections, keep this definition in mind because it acts as a good barometer for the type of relationship you want. So, what makes a strong critical connection?

First, as we discussed earlier, strong connections are more than networking. The coaching clients I have worked with who started their vision statements with everything they wanted or needed to gain from cultivating critical connections, for the most part had the mindset that if they meet their quotas and follow the corporate policies, then the outcome will result in a promotion. And for some, that type of philosophy has held true. They have done their networking duty at the work social functions and didn't go much beyond that. That may work for some people, but if you are reading this book that isn't the case for you. Most people who put their time in at Thursday evening cocktail hour still find themselves unable to make meaningful connections.

The real key is meaningful connections with mutual intentions. A strong critical connection is both reciprocated and authentic, but I don't like relying on the word "authentic" because it implies that the relationships you are in now are either inauthentic or disingenuous, and I don't believe that is the case. Instead, they may simply lack a conscious awareness and empathetic purpose. I liken it to going to a job fair when you are desperate for a job. HR professionals can sense when you are saying exactly what they want to hear rather than answering truthfully. The same thing is true of networking. The people you are trying to connect with can tell if you aren't being yourself, or if you are only talking to them because of the position they hold or opportunity they may have. They probably experience it all the time.

This brings us to another important element to a critical connection—intention. Remember, the purpose of your connections should be aimed at mutual benefits; you cannot do that without knowing your intention. If you are approaching a connection with anything less than your own truth, whatever that means for you, then you will struggle to ever form a trustworthy relationship in which you can both rely on each other.

To cultivate critical connections means that you and another willing (and I stress willing) person, department, company, or business have made a meaningful and conscious connection in which there are mutual benefits. It is important to note here that if the other party is unwilling to play a significant role in a relationship of any kind, they have already forged a barrier that blocks all opportunities for expansion with you, both professionally and personally. An unwilling participant will simply view the connection as passive, one that isn't critical enough to be of benefit, much like those who recognize that you are not being authentic in your interactions.

Cultivating critical connections incorporates the practice of cultivating relationships, the investigation of what's critical (authentic), and the commitment and effort required to keep those connections intact. The heart of a critical connection is finding meaning, empathy, consciousness, truthfulness, trustworthiness among two willing participants. Which in turn leads to the essential goals of forming a critical connection of growing as a professional, developing skills, and furthering your career. Whether this takes the form of a recommendation for a position you are applying to or being asked to lead a seminar, the specifics of your connecting goals will be different but should be grounded in a growth mindset.

What is the Mindful Connector Method™?

Relationship building isn't a new concept to our society; professionals have long discussed and developed new and better ways to effectivly build relationships. The program I have laid out in this book, the Mindful Connector Method™, brings these abstract concepts and the soft skills involved in relationship building and fits them neatly into easily applicable, concrete guidelines.

When I worked on the yearlong mentoring program helping college students connect with executive level professionals, I recognized that these skills were lacking on both sides of the coin and I really had to do some soul searching into my own natural affinity for making connections to figure out how to teach a traditionally abstract concept in a concrete and easy to disseminate way. I said to myself, "I have to cultivate critical connections." From that, my entire philosophy developed.

The Mindful Connector Method™ is a strong tool. It's fun and insightful, and if practiced on a regular basis, it can elevate your level of communication and confidence in building authentic connections in ways that can provide rewards from school years through to retirement. The great thing about the Mindful Connector Method™ is that once you have started working on it, the techniques apply to every situation you are in.

Here's why I believe cultivating critical connections gets to the heart of the issue. When you think "critical," something happens in your heart and mind. "Critical" denotes vital, significant, decisive, and serious. You can't dismiss the implications of the word.

There are three steps involved in cultivating critical connections. In step one, Cultivate, you will learn how to prepare yourself for the relationship you wish to build and how to lay the groundwork when beginning any relationship. In step two, Critical, you will learn the steps for evaluating your relationships and determining the value you can bring to them. In step three, Connections, you will learn how to foster and further build your relationships. Each stage along the way includes important elements that help you quickly grasp the concepts and learn how to successfully apply them in your life.

Chapter Two

STEP 1. CULTIVATE

*The single greatest "people skill" is a highly developed & authentic interest in the *other* person.*

– Bob Burg

Imagine a farmer who is preparing the soil for planting seeds to harvest when the summer comes. As spring arrives and the first buds start popping through the dirt, the crop will either be plentiful or meager and fail. The outcome, of course, depends upon how that farmer primed the soil and fostered his seeds. The same is true of our relationships. The outcome and health of our relationships depends on how we cultivate them.

One definition of cultivate says, "to promote or improve the growth of a plant, crop, etc. by labor and attention." Another defines it, "to develop or improve by education or training; train; refine."[3] Both of these definitions are useful when we start thinking about this initial step toward better relationships. It is your job to promote growth by working hard and focusing your attention while also learning and refining.

This first element of the Mindful Connector Method™ requires significant upfront effort, strategy, and planning, in other words, preparing the ground for planting. During the cultivating season of your professional relationship building, it's essential that you create a vision for connecting—your

Connections Intention Vision (CIV) Statement, for how and why making specific critical connections is important. It's your roadmap.

Take a few minutes right now to jot down your initial CIV.

My initial CIV...

In the next section of this chapter, we will work on refining and focusing this statement, but the differences between this first draft and your final version will give you marching orders for your own connecting process.

As you begin this initial step toward stronger, more productive connections, keep a few things in the forefront of your mind. Your focus should be on mutual benefit. Cultivating mutual benefit requires an openness to change, an ability to listen, and a willingness to tune in to the needs of others.

Imagine that you are planting a seed in which the harvest will be shared by both you and the people you are connecting with. If it is bountiful, there will be plenty of shared benefit to go around.

Part 1: Prepare the ground for your connections

The first part of the cultivation step requires you to do a bit of self-reflection. Before you jump into trying to cultivate critical connections, you first must understand yourself and your intentions. Reflect on your motives, prepare to re-evaluate your communications, emphasize a positivity mindset, and learn to recognize appropriate opportunities. This is what the CIV statement is all about. Writing down your Connections Intention Vision Statement helps to make it a clear goal with actionable purpose.

Your Connections Intention Vision (CIV) Statement

Before meeting or connecting with people, you should reflect on your motives. Every social situation, be it personal or professional, big or small, should be entered into with intention and forethought. That isn't to imply that every interaction should be highly orchestrated, but rather that you are prepared mentally for navigating a crowd or talking to strangers in a genuine way.

Too often we find ourselves in situations that we are not prepared for, which means we fall back on familiar routines rather than working on the new skills in order to cultivate critical connections. Going into social situations with clear intentions and purpose allows you to move more freely instead of forcing an interaction or letting anxiety dictate your decisions.

Let's go back to that Connections Intention Vision (CIV) Statement that you wrote at the beginning of this chapter. Creating a clear vision statement or CIV serves as a guide during networking situations of all kinds, keeping you focused on the end goal. This approach will also help you weed out most of the connections that won't be critical to your development.

Your CIV Statement provides:

- a vision that will guide your connections
- a road map to aid in navigating a sea of never-ending opportunities for connecting
- a way for you to become laser focused on your intentions for making a connection and ultimately determine the quality of the connections you make
- an ever-evolving resource, which you should always be reworking, retooling, and refining

Revising your CIV statement

Take a look at the statement you wrote earlier. Does it accomplish everything listed above? Is it appropriately focused on mutual benefits? Does it speak to your own personal definition of what a successful critical connection looks like? In other words, your CIV Statement should not be vague, such as, "Making critical connections will help me do better at work." The problems in that statement are two-fold. The first is that what a strong critical connection looks like isn't defined. The second is that the motive is purely self-centered.

As you begin to revise your CIV Statement, start with a simple list of the reasons you want to make critical connections. As we have talked about before (but it is worth repeating) your purpose should be one of mutual benefit. Think about what you could gain from critical connections, but also consider how others might benefit from having critical connections with you.

This isn't something we often spend a lot of time thinking about, but I warned you, this step requires self-reflection. Spend some time thinking about what you personally bring to the table. What you bring to your connections may vary depending on the connection. For example, if your potential connection has an interest in golf and you are a skilled golfer, maybe you bring a love of golf and some pointers to the relationship. Other times it may be other mutual connections, or something work related. In order to better understand what mutual benefit your connection might get out of a relationship with you, you have to improve your communication skills (more on that later). For now, it is enough to reflect on your own strengths as an individual and as a professional.

Now it is time to rewrite your CIV Statement. Make sure that it is no more than 200 words or two to three sentences. Remember, you want to use this almost like a mantra, something to guide you while you are working through this cultivating step. For right now, your CIV can be vague (remember, you will be revising this as you learn and grow). It can be as simple as, "My goal is to cultivate deeper, more truthful relationships to help others achieve their goals." Keep in mind that the idea is to write a meaningful statement that describes what critical connections will mean to you.

My revised CIV...

As you revise, create a picture in your mind of exactly what these connections you are trying to make look like. What does a successful connection look like? Spend some time here with this question. Revisit the first chapter where we talked about "What Makes a Strong Critical Connection?" Don't simply be a passive reader. Visualize how the definition of strong critical connections applies to you and to those around you.

Once your CIV Statement is ready and you begin to live it out, you'll notice a return on investment in the form of solid relationships. Consider the Pareto Principle[4], also known as the 80–20 rule, the law of the vital few, or the principle of factor sparsity. It states that, for many events, roughly 80 percent of the effects come from 20 percent of the causes. In other words, when we focus on the goals or actions that would make the greatest impact, we can limit our output while still reaping the benefits. That is the goal of the cultivating step. When you consider the 80–20 rule, cultivating is the 20 percent that will bring you 80 percent of your success in your relationship connections.

Dedicating 20 percent of your relationship-building time to a quality effort in preparing your soil through reflection about your motives, writing out that vision in your CIV Statement, and living out the mission of that statement, will almost guarantee 80 percent of your success.

Recognize Opportunities

Once you have crafted your CIV Statement, it's time to put it to work. Be strategic. Not every networking or social event is the right ground for meeting people or building critical relationships. It's imperative that you mindfully choose your opportunities to connect and know what your motives are going in. Mindfully choosing opportunities to connect means you should always ask yourself, "What is my purpose for attending a particular networking or social event?"

Having an answer to that question and knowing your purpose keeps you on target for your intended mission, which should be to create genuine relationships that will help in your transformation or growth. You will be less likely to be swept up by the mood of the room if you have your intention at the forefront and realistic expectations about what the networking environment will look like for you.

Remember that you're hoping to cultivate critical connections, so if you're having a bad day or you have an energy of desperation to find a job, you either need to shift your energy to a more positive state or simply stay home. I guarantee it makes a difference. It doesn't make sense to waste your energy and time attending social or business networking in a negative state of mind. So, make sure you have a CIV Statement, a purpose, and the right energy before going in. And last but not least, remember that when you are looking to make critical connections, keyword being critical, quantity is not valued over quality.

In My Bubble of Positivity

In the last section, I mentioned shifting your energy to a more positive state. For some people, this may be uncomfortable. And some may even be saying to themselves, "I am here to make business connections, not to make friends." To that I say stay in your bubble of positivity.

I kept myself in a bubble of positivity for many years during my career. In dealing with so many variations of systemic racism in the workplace, maintaining a bubble of positivity kept me sane and will do the same for you. It allowed me the wherewithal to maintain my critical connections over time. I recognized early on that your energy and the energy of others plays a big role in the success or failure of relationships. If you enter a space, situation or scenario with a negative energy, then the space, the people in it, the events that happen there, will all meet your energy and the interactions will turn out exactly as you expected—poorly.

That bubble of positivity that I speak about is a place where only positive influences and thoughts are allowed to reside. What I know for sure is that what you put in is what comes out.

I will share a short example of a workplace situation in which I had to stand firm in that bubble of positivity and not give in to the negative vibes that were definitely being directed at me. In the end, it garnered a short-lived connection. So, here's how it went down in summary. I had just started a new job. I was introduced to my supervisor and immediately recognized a negative energy that was unpleasant and even hostile. I imagined that she may have had a chip on her shoulder or didn't want me there. I had my thoughts about why—the color of my skin. Maybe I wasn't her first choice for the job; she didn't think I was qualified enough. I decided to give her the benefit of the doubt. I had been hired because of a critical connection I had developed years ago, after all. How was I supposed to handle this situation? How would you handle it if you found yourself in my situation?

I'm sure you have experienced other people's negative thoughts, actions and views, but we each have a choice in how we react. It's how we manage the negative that affects our outlook, how others perceive us, our ability to make connections, and the strength of our bubble of positivity.

The situation with my supervisor never got better. It only seemed to go from bad to worse as the chip on her shoulder and my black face didn't go away. When I was challenged with this situation in a new job, it was a game-changing moment for me. This particular instance released an unseen power in me that set the tone for how I would deal with future challenging situations in business, my career, and in my personal life.

One day she asked me to prepare and deliver a presentation for a major corporation, and I was given noticeably short notice. My supervisor was supposed to do it but opted out at the last minute. I can be spontaneous on occasion, but few people like being surprised with a situation in which people are counting on them and they have little or no time to prepare. I pictured myself standing in front of the corporation without my notes in order or a presentation to show. Unfortunately, I didn't have a choice so, a little annoyed, I took on the challenge and put together the best presentation I could with the information I had. I asked my supervisor if I could defer to her if I got to a point in the presentation that I didn't feel confident enough to deliver. "Sure," she said. "I can take care of that." I took her reassurance to heart and was confident that the presentation would go off without a hitch because she was going to back me if I needed it.

On the day of the meeting, I was in a good head space as is often my state of mind. The meeting began and I launched into my presentation. All was well until we reached that very section where I needed help. I looked over to my supervisor and asked her, "Can you offer any insights into this area for everyone here today?" She said, "NO. I don't have anything to offer. You can handle it."

Well, NO I couldn't handle it because I didn't have any in-depth knowledge into that area and was looking to her for help. I kept my eyes intent upon her for what felt like a lifetime. It was like pigs being led out to slaughter and she didn't flinch. Though I managed not to show it, I was so upset I wasn't sure what to do. I don't like to be embarrassed and I felt that my supervisor was enjoying every moment of seeing me cringe. To be honest, I believe that was her intent. This wasn't the first time nor would it be the last my supervisor put me in a difficult, unexpected, and embarrassing situation. She seemed to be set on testing my resolve.

However, there was positive energy in the room. A colleague from my company (not black) quickly pulled me out of my "what the hell is going on here?" state by calmly saying, "Go ahead, Monique. Just move on to the next point in the presentation and get back to them later." Meanwhile, all the questions could have been answered immediately by my supervisor. I don't know why this particular undercut was such a big moment for me. What I do know is that there was a lot of negative energy boiling up inside. I had a choice to make, go low or stay high. We all experience pain, but suffering is a choice! I wasn't going to give her the pleasure.

It isn't always easy staying within that bubble of positivity. My heart was heavy that day, really heavy. Staying positive in a world full of daily negative energy was intense. Every day I felt that I was being tested to prove my skills and abilities. I wasn't quite sure why I was being singled out, but I knew I had to respond to my situation differently. Deep inside I had a knowing that I would be rewarded later for responding respectfully as opposed to what she may have expected of me, giving her more fuel.

In the end, I decided to approach my daily drama as a ritual of taking the high road—no matter what. I changed my mindset and viewed it as a stepping stone and a way to develop my character so that I could step into something greater, later. I wrapped positivity around myself like a protective shield.

I knew if I wanted positive outcomes from this experience, I had to think, act, and respond well above my negative circumstances. In the end, there was a huge bonus; that same supervisor who had previously caused me so much emotional anguish became a short-lived critical connection. I learned quite a bit about myself and how character can be built under pressure. Though I didn't keep that job, my reputation stayed intact, and I developed a great resource who gave me access to information and connections. Lesson learned: Stay in that bubble of positivity.

Elevate Your Communications

In the introduction I talked about the simple method I created to help people practice how they cultivate the critical connections they had made. The Mindful Connector Method™ helps you elevate your communications with the people you're trying to build strong connections to. Communication is the crux of any solid connection. Good communication requires you to listen (really hear what the other person is trying to say), speak, and write well. These three pillars form the foundation for great communication and subsequently forming and maintaining critical connections. I know it may seem trite, but how you communicate makes a world of difference.

Remember that the first impression you make is crucial. The beginning of every connection starts with that first impression. It may sound a bit cliché, but if we don't practice and perfect our communication skills as we continue to build authentic connections, it will be harder to master the Mindful Connector Method™.

The next time you are out in public, whether you are just grabbing a cup of coffee, going to work, or picking up some groceries, look around. How many people are connecting around you? How many are staring at a device? The recent trend in school is that children are no longer learning cursive writing because it is considered a dying art. People are relying on texting and social media as their outlets for communicating. We are simultaneously gaining more instant and constant access to other people while at the same time growing further and further apart. Text messaging has grown by 23 percent since 2016[4]. Americans send about 26 billion texts a day! That means we are losing crucial skills and craving that real face-to-face communication that we once had. I believe there will come a day when we as a society will wish we were spending more time communicating face to face and through writing. We will long for personal connections and for connecting in the traditional formats.

Have you ever run into an issue in which you try to communicate an idea through text or email and the person on the receiving end completely misinterprets your tone, intention or message, possibly resulting in a disagreement, conflict, or a lot of extra back and forth communication? If so, you are far from alone. Imagine now if this miscommunication happened with a fledgling connection. It would put a strain on the fragile foundation of your new connection.

Your ability to write, speak, listen, and present yourself in a coherent and professional manner matters a lot. You will be judged by the way you communicate. Your advancement and connection opportunities will be closely tied to your communication skills. To make connections, you've got to step into an environment with something that sets you apart. You've got to be able to establish instant rapport.

Listening

We talk about the skill of listening first because it doesn't matter what else you do while communicating if you aren't listening. You could be the best orator and a *New York Times* bestselling author, but if you aren't listening, your connection won't get off the ground. This goes back to your motivation for connecting and your CIV Statement. If your motivation for cultivating critical connections is to be mutually beneficial to the people you are connecting with (and by now it should be!) then you need to know the other person—you do that by listening.

Approach each conversation with the goal of learning something new. Whether it is about the person you are talking to or some tidbit of knowledge they may share, if your focus is on learning, you will be more apt to listen carefully. While you are listening, take the time to give cues that you are listening. This can be nodding your head or asking open-ended follow-up questions.

Speaking

Speaking, of course, is the next important skill to master when you are preparing to cultivate critical connections. Speaking well has a twofold meaning. First, you should be articulate, with correct gramar and sentence structure. You should pronounce words correctly and avoid too much slang. I am not suggesting to not be yourself, but it is important to consider how others perceive you (it may require some code-switching).[5] If you speak to business colleagues the same way you speak to your friends, you may come off as unprofessional, too casual, or even uneducated.

The second part of speaking well is thoughtful consideration of what you are going to say in order to contribute constructively and creatively to the conversation. There is a reason for the saying, "Think before you speak." When you join in conversations, make sure that you have already utilized your listening skills to best understand the person you are speaking to. Be sure to have an array of topics ready that you can talk about if the conversation lags. To that end, keep yourself up on world news and current events so you can engage in discourse.

It is important when forging new connections that you always have something to say, but that something has to be relevant and you have to say it in a way that commands attention and respect. Along with being able to carry on a conversation, it is equally as important that you are able to express your needs and ask for what you want in your critical connection. Earlier in this book, I spoke about five college students being paired with C-level executives in mentor-mentee relationships. These students didn't know how to ask for what they desired in their relationships with their mentors. They lacked the necessary confidence to ask for what they wanted, so the opportunity to expand and grow their connections actually presented a challenge for them. It wasn't until they learned these important skills that they were able to cultivate those connections.

Your Writing Abilities

I won't go into specifics about writing; this isn't a book about grammar, but how you express yourself in writing is important. It's awkward and unprofessional to send a note to one of your critical connections on your smartphone in text slang or to send an email full of grammatical errors. It's not impressive and may even be off-putting to certain connections. Your ability to write professionally can be linked to how much you are reading. I constantly read a wide variety of books: novels, personal development books, and textbooks. Reading helps me improve my writing and my verbal skills, so try to make it a daily habit.

Part 2: Plant Your Seeds

The second part of the cultivation process starts after an authentic relationship has been formed and there is a mutual agreement between the two parties that the relationship is valuable enough to nurture. This is when you start to plant your seeds so that your new connections can begin to grow. The seeds you plant are the ones that will make your connections flourish. Of course, you may be wondering what kinds of seeds I am planting to nurture a relationship if I am not trying to grow vegetables. Well, the seeds we are talking about here are the efforts you make to improve the trust, commitment, and benefits of your connections. These include actively getting to know your connections, allowing yourself to be open so others can get to know you, fostering commonalities, and of course, time and patience.

First, put in the time to get to know your connection's values, beliefs, and desires. All of us are guided by these three determining factors. When you understand someone's values, beliefs, and desires, you understand both who they are and if they are someone who would bring value to your life.

The second requires allowing your critical connection to find out more about you and the value in your connection. It can be all too easy in a semi-social business-type setting to put up barriers and only let others see your professional side. This goes back to our purpose for participating in these types of events. When the purpose is to network, we may fall back on our fake smiles and meaningless small talk, feeling pressure to be the perfect little worker. But when our purpose is to find a meaningful connection with others, that pressure lightens because it is less about the quantity of connections we make or the number of business cards we leave with and more about the quality of those connections. Rather than rushing through the room with your brightest smile, you can take your time with each person you meet and be open and honest.

Both sides of this equation are equally important. On one hand, getting to know your connection helps you better understand if it is a connection that will be mutually beneficial. On the other hand, allowing your critical connection to get to know you provides the same thing. For many who are not used to making these kinds of critical connections, it can be difficult at first to allow others to get to know you. We have a tendency to remain guarded and present a façade of what we think the other person wants to see rather than allowing them to get to know the real us. If you have hopes of creating authentic and trustworthy relationships, however, it is important that you are honest and up front while you are planting the seeds of your relationship. Remind yourself of your goals in the process of cultivating critical connections.

These efforts take time. If you think of a farmer tending his crop, you realize that after the seeds are planted there's still much to be done before you see a sprout popping up out of the land. The same applies to the seeds you plant as you form critical connections.

Assess your connections

Once you have begun getting to know the people you are socializing with, it is time to assess the connection. The first question you need to ask is, "If this connection continues, will there be a mutual benefit?" Ask yourself what you bring to that specific relationship and what the other person brings, too. Decide if this is a balanced relationship that meets your expectations.

Next, you have to decide if the other person agrees that there is value in it for them. The answer may not be self-evident in the initial phase of the cultivating stage, but you will sense whether or not there is a conscious effort from both sides. If you're not sitting around waiting months to hear from your critical connections, then you can make the reasonable assumption that they're making an effort, too.

If both parties are responsive to emails, social media, and phone calls, I would venture to say you have conscious effort on each side. Typically, the person with the most leadership qualities, experience, corporate status, and business acumen is not the cultivator of the relationship. The eighteen to twenty-five-year-old or the individual who has more to gain than to offer from a critical connection will most likely play the role of the cultivator.

Most of the time, it's a one-sided affair because both parties don't have the same needs and desires at stake or the same intention for making the critical connection. If both parties involved have similar CIVs, then it's an automatic win-win; however, that's rarely the case. So, the cultivator has to do most of the work, which leads us to the second step in the Mindful Connector Method™: investigating the Critical.

Make Time for Practice

Here's an exercise to try out.

When you go to your next networking or social gathering, don't take any business cards. Instead, make your purpose for attending this event about helping someone else make a critical connection by inquiring and listening to their reasons for being there.

When you finally meet someone who has a story to tell—and they all do—it's okay to take their business card and reconnect at a later date, but remember this exercise is not about you.

By the way, exchanging business cards at an event, just because, doesn't mean you've made a real connection. You haven't made a critical connection. Cultivating critical connections is going to take some practice and sacrifice. It's the reason the Mindful Connector Method™ was created.

Chapter Three

STEP 2. CRITICAL

I've learned that people will forget what you've said, people will forget what you did, but people will never forget how you made them feel.

– Maya Angelou

I like to call the Critical step the process of finding the life of your connection. After you have cultivated your relationship by preparing the soil and planting your seeds of expansion, you'll have to put some thought into your next course of action. Your newfound relationship should be qualified by determining the critical factors that make your relationship mutually beneficial. If you have taken the steps set forth up until this point, you should be well on your way to recognizing the power of mutual benefit.

When qualifying the critical factors in your relationship, you'll want to understand what is meaningful to the other person. Find out what makes the relationship valuable for the other person and make that a gauge for the pulse of your connection. This step focuses on the intentional value you can bring to the relationship. In other words, what's in it for them?

I consider this the unselfish step of the Mindful Connector Method™. This is the part most people struggle with and failure to do it well is the reason some relationships dissolve. When networking or mingling socially, the natural inclination for most people is to approach an opportunity to connect with the hopes of gaining something for themselves from the other person. You either have some immediate or desperate need, or someone has information and status from which you hope to benefit. The problem with that approach is that you've failed to make your connection about the other person. We have talked about this before, but the danger here is that your relationship may be shallow, forced or disingenuous which, needless to say, doesn't foster the long lasting, valuable relationships we are working toward in this book.

The Mindful Connector Method™ teaches the reverse of that self-interested plan of attack with good reason. We have all heard the saying, "When you give, you get." We don't often give a lot of thought to this phrase but when we do it sounds almost paradoxical. But the truth is, your connections will be more willing to be generous with their time, skills, and support when you have cultivated a critical connection based on giving. **Mastering the selfless side of your relationships is where the real power lies.**

It is important to note here that while the critical step is an unselfish step, that does not mean that you must be entirely selfless in your relationships. Understanding what you gain from your connections helps prevent you from becoming a doormat in the effort to make other people happy. Instead, this step is simply about taking a moment to make sure that you step outside of yourself to view yourself the way others might see you while finding the critical factor for your connection.

There is no hard and fast, one-size-fits-all rule that I can give you to help you qualify your connections and determine how the other person will find value in connecting with you. That is something you must take the time to determine on your own, but understanding what you bring to the relationship allows you to move forward with intention.

There are two things you can look for to help you gauge the critical in your relationships. The first and most important thing to do is to find out if the connection is equally advantageous. It doesn't mean you have to match the status and qualifications of your connection one-for-one, but you both have to agree that the connection is important enough to put in the effort to stay connected.

Secondly, when you realize the life that can be garnered from the relationship, you'll spend more time cultivating it. Discerning the life in a relationship means that you can clearly see that there is a vital progression of growth and development. It means that two people can exchange value for value to some extent. In essence, the relationship will thrive because it is deemed crucial enough that each person will contribute substance to it so that it remains alive.

Determining the Critical

So, how do you determine the critical or the life of your connection?

1. **Start by having the courage to ask yourself, "What is my intent, and what can I offer to my connection that will be of significance to him or her in our mutual arrangement?"** I suggest spending some time with this question. It is easy to both underestimate and overestimate what you bring to a relationship. Sometimes the critical factor that you have to offer varies based on the person you are connecting to. Be honest with yourself about your strengths, skills, and attributes.

   Keep in mind that the value you have to offer may not be the same types of things that others have to offer you. If you are cultivating a critical connection to a CEO of your company who wields decision-making power, in-depth knowledge of your field, and the ability to elevate your position in the company, the value you add to the connection probably won't be on par. You cannot offer to introduce him to important people or teach him about a field he is already familiar with, but that doesn't mean you have nothing to offer.

   It reminds me of my experience introducing inexperienced students to CIOs. Just because the students were new to the field didn't mean that they had nothing to offer.

Knowing what you have to offer and what you can provide for others gives you power. Rather than being at the mercy of the CIOs and higher-ups, you can act with purpose while making your connections. Maybe that is simply a reliable support person, perhaps it is common interests, perhaps it is your ability to cultivate critical connections.

Think about what others gain from forming connections with you and make a list if that helps you visualize your connections better.

2. **Next, determine whether there is a mutual agreement as to whether your relationship has meaning.** You may not be able to get an initial response; it may take a few tries to find out if there is a mutual agreement. But it's imperative that you acquire the information so you don't waste your energy cultivating the wrong relationship.

   For example, I've had a long-standing critical connection with a CEO-level executive for many years. One for one, there is nothing I can distinctly see that makes our relationship mutually beneficial. I've facilitated the relationship by being the person who makes most of the effort to keep our connection intact. I know that if I were to assess the critical nature of this relationship at this stage in my development, I would find that it feeds more of my critical needs than his.

Here's why it's important for me to stay critically connected. He was the first person who made me feel worthy, and in my early twenties, I was looking to be validated in the corporate arena. If there ever comes a time when the other person in this relationship stops responding to my efforts to reach out or my desire to stay connected, then I will conclude that the lifeline in this critical connection is over.

3. **Finally, there may come a time when you will have to decide whether or not you should continue to pursue a relationship that isn't feeding your personal and professional expansion.** For all you know, it may not be working for the other person in the connection either. Give yourself permission to honestly assess critical connections and leave relationships that are not serving you if that is the conclusion you come to.

   Don't take it personally. Your efforts will be better spent on cultivating critical connections where your mutual agreement is solid and long lasting.

Once you have determined the critical factors of your connections, you are ready to move on to the third step. Keep in mind that cultivating critical connections is not about racing to the finish line. In fact, there are no finish lines when it comes to your connections, as you will learn in the next step. Take whatever time you need moving through this second step because while you did most of the heavy lifting in step one, finding the critical is vital to determine the future of a connection, understanding your connections better, and knowing how to maintain connection.

chapter four

STEP 3. CONNECTIONS

I speak to everyone in the same way, whether he is the garbage man or the president of the university.

– Albert Einstein.

This step of the relationship-building process is the Connected stage. How you stay connected is just as important as how you cultivate relationships and how you determine the critical value a relationship can bring to an individual or business. The ways in which you maintain your relationships will determine the longevity of those connections.

Essentially, the way we stay connected comes down to the balance we find between social media and in-person communication. There is no cut and dry, right or wrong answer, but in my experience, it is important to avoid relying too heavily on social media as your only way of keeping in touch. A lot is lost through the buffer of technology.

Over the years, the way we sustain our critical relationships will evolve. With the continuous evolution of the internet and social media, there should be no reason for relationships to fail entirely, but when cultivating critical connections, relying on social media alone to stay connected and continue to build your relationships may not cut it. Relationships based on social media often lead to less beneficial, substantive and trustworthy relationships; instead they become more superficial, routine, and distant.

Traditional ways of connecting are still very important and are a more intimate way to connect with others. That doesn't mean that there isn't a place for social media. Personal notes, lunch meetings, networking events, and phone calls, coupled with new media, are a powerful combination. Depending on your age and other factors, how you prefer to stay connected will vary. You can augment whatever platform you've decided to use by combining efforts. As I mentioned before, there is no one best way, just the right way for you and your critical connections.

Social Media

Social media has become unavoidable as individuals and businesses adopt it in wide use. Most people use one form of social media or another to stay in touch with family, reconnect with high school acquaintances, find local events, promote businesses, or network with new and potential connections. Social media is alluring as it provides the opportunity for instant and ongoing connectedness. When you are using it during the Mindful Connector Method™, do so mindfully and with purpose. Keep in mind your purpose for connecting that we talked about in the very beginning of the book. Social media can provide a quick and easy way to learn more about your connection, stay up to date with their lives, stay relevant, and keep your name in their mind. Remember, social media is a tool, not an outcome in and of itself.

In other words, when you are interacting on social media, don't assume that a like, comment or share is the equivalent of a connection. Rather, those online interactions are support for a connection that you are also building through in-person interactions. Most critical connections expect that you will stay in touch through technology, so taking the time to learn how to effectively use Facebook, LinkedIn, Twitter, and other social media platforms to meet expectations and maximize your reach has become the new norm.

Empowering In-Person Connections

There is a power to in-person connections that doesn't exist in the same way with social media relationships. While you may get to know each other's interests or see each other's hobbies, social media lacks a personal comradery. I want to be able to look my connections square in the eye because that's how I can sense their energy.

With all of the social media tools available for staying connected, don't forget the influence you can have by taking someone to lunch or going out for a game of golf. **These traditional means of keeping your relationships intact, in this age, will be the stuff that takes your connection from casual to meaningful.** The age, skills, and preferences of the person you've made a critical connection with will dictate how you should use different traditional and digital tools.

If you have determined a connection is worth maintaining, take the necessary steps to connect on both social media and in person. This can be as simple as getting coffee every other week, taking a walk together on your lunch break, or going out for drinks on the weekend. Regardless of what your in-person connections look like, take responsibility for making them happen. Don't wait for your connection to set the pace or lay the groundwork. Remember, you are following the Mindful Connector Method™, but you don't know what kind of connecting skills the other person comes to the table with. If you want the connection, make it happen.

Making a Plan

Equally as important as knowing how you will connect is having a plan of action to make sure staying connected doesn't become another pipe dream that you don't follow through with. There are key elements to your connection strategy: type of approach, touch point, length of relationship, and lifeline.

Type of Approach refers to how you will stay in contact with that person. Be as specific and clear as possible. As your plan starts filling up with more and more contacts, you will appreciate the quick reference sheet for the best way to stay in touch with each one.

Touch point refers to how often you should be reaching out or following up. Your touch point may be different for each different type of connection. For example, if you have one connection that you meet with for coffee and interact with on LinkedIn, you won't do those two things with the same frequency. You may only do coffee quarterly but like, share, and comment on LinkedIn twice a week.

Length of time in the relationship helps you keep track of your connections and helps you continually assess and reassess the critical factor and the best ways to connect. As time goes on and the relationship is stable, you may be able to change the touch points making them less frequent or move over more to social media.

Lifeline refers to the role that person plays in your life along with the critical factor that makes your relationship mutually beneficial or at the very least, the benefit you gain. This is another way to continually follow up on steps one and two of the Mindful Connector Method™. As time passes, reassess the critical aspect of the relationships.

The Mindful Connector Method™ approach to connectedness is simple and having tools to assist you makes it even better. I developed the Connection Strategy Grid (CSG) to help you manage, at a glance, how you stay connected to your critical connections. The CSG requires you to populate each zone with the name, type of approach (social media/ traditional), touch point (how often), length (of time in your relationship), and lifeline (the critical factor that makes your relationship mutually beneficial or just beneficial for you) for each person that you consider a critical connection.

Use the CSG to help get you started. You may want to keep a grid of your own on the computer or in a notebook as you develop more connections.

My CSG

Name of connection	Mike Buckman	
Type of connection	Traditional (lunch and Coffee)	
Touch point	Bi-annual	
Length of relationship	18 years	
Lifeline	Mentor (C-level)	
Telephone	(222)555-1100	
Email	mike@email.com	

Chapter five

GOLDner NUGGETS FOR BECOMING A MASTER CONNECTOR

It takes 20 years to build a reputation and five minutes to ruin it. If you think about that, you'll do things differently.

– Warren Buffett

My friend Greg Goldner knows the secret to making meaningful connections. He is a master communicator and an expert connector. The insights he offers in this chapter are truly gold nuggets to help ramp up your connections.

By Greg Goldner

"How did he get in touch with her? She's the executive vice-president!"

"Seriously, she got that job? I didn't even think she was all that qualified for it."

"I'd love to get in touch with someone at that company, but how?"

These conversations happen every day between people of all ages and job titles and in all areas of the professional world. Whether we know it or not, somewhere inside of all of us is the ability to network like a badass! For our purposes, let's call that badass a "master connector."

So, what's a master connector? Cool, I'm glad you asked.

A master connector is a person with an insanely deep contact list. This person can pick up their iPhone and get in touch with almost anyone, or at least within one connection of almost anyone.

But what if I'm not outgoing? What if I don't know how to network? What if I don't have time? I've heard all these things before, and none of them can hold you back from becoming a master connector. Don't believe me? Read this section and then call me a liar.

ITS ALL ABOUT WHO YOU KNOW!

Whether you're trying to get floor tickets to a Drake concert or you're hoping your resume is on the top of the stack, it's all about who you know. Who can you get in touch with that can help you get those tickets? Who do you know at (insert company name here) that can make sure the hiring manager looks at your resume early in the process?

Let's put it in terms of advancing your career, which is probably why you're reading this book in the first place.

You could have the most impressive resume to go along with a unique list of extracurricular activities, but if you don't have a contact, it really doesn't matter. Now, I'm not saying that a resume doesn't matter, because it does, a lot. It doesn't matter who your connection is if you don't have the background that a prospective employer requires.

Look at this process in two parts, with the ultimate goal of getting an interview. Build your resume to the best it can possibly be and find the best possible contact for the job you are going after.

The first step is up to you: Build your resume and make yourself a rock star candidate. The second step is what this book is ALL about… making those CRITICAL CONNECTIONS!

How do you make a contact and build your network?

You never know when you're going to meet someone who will change your life. The girl at the party who becomes your wife. The man on the plane who happens to be the CEO of a Fortune 500 company. The guy who found your glass slipper that you lost at the ball the night before. Okay, Cinderella, you get the picture.

It's critical to stay in contact with the people you meet because you never know if and when they will play a vital role in your career. For the most part, when it comes to parties, work functions, and dinner with friends, I always do my best to say yes. I do this for multiple reasons, but as I said before, you never know who you're going to meet. And for the most part, your connections will come through family, friends, or acquaintances. Rarely will you ever blindly email someone or connect with them on LinkedIn and be able to legitimately add them to your network. And to be clear, your network isn't all of your connections on LinkedIn or the thousands of best friends you have on Facebook or Instagram. Your network are those individuals you can call on to get you the Drake concert tickets or to make sure the hiring manager checks out your resume.

Connections can be made virtually anywhere, so when it comes to meeting people, don't be afraid to extend yourself and don't forget to follow up. If you reach out to someone and they don't reciprocate, what happens? You're in the same spot you were before. No harm done! But most likely you will get some sort of response, whether a conversation in person or an email. Once that happens, congrats, you've got the ball rolling.

Why Are Connections Important?

Connections will open doors that you didn't know opened and will introduce you to people you never dreamed of meeting; these can become your greatest assets. Think of a contact as a hammer in your toolbox. Anyone who's ever done anything handy knows that you can't do a whole lot without a hammer. Your connections are your hammers!

If one hundred resumes come in for a job, a connection can make sure that your resume sits on top of the pile. A contact can give you an added advantage by vouching for you and letting a hiring manager know, "Yeah, I know her. She's a really hard worker and has a great personality. You should definitely take a good look at her resume."

So now you've got the strong resume and one of your contacts has put in a good word for you. If I were the hiring manager, I'd probably be calling you right now.

Do you see what you did here? You had a great resume (step 1), you had the contact (step 2), and you got the interview. Bingo!

Your Connections and Who They Know

When you add a critical connection to your network, you're not just adding them, you're adding their network of connections as well.

Here's what I'm talking about. I'm telling Monique about a job I really want and Monique says, "You should talk to my friend Jane. She used to work there."

It's that simple! And believe me, it really is that easy.

Your LinkedIn profile shows your direct connections and then shows your network. Your network is your connections, plus the connections others have—same concept. If you don't know what I'm referring to, then you probably don't have a LinkedIn profile. If that's the case, stop reading this book right now and go create one. LinkedIn is an essential tool for networking and becoming a master connector (but I'll touch on this later). It's almost a guarantee that your success will rarely be about your direct contacts and much more about who they know. That's fine because all you need is a foot in the door—also known as the inside edge.

Keep this in mind: When you add a critical connection to your network, you're not just directly adding them, you're adding their network of connections as well.

A Master Connector's Million-Dollar Secret . . . Shhhhh!

When reaching out to someone you hope to add to your network, the keyword to use is "advice." If you flat out ask for a job, they are going to be extremely turned off. Why? Because they don't know you well enough to vouch for you, and it also seems like you have a sense of entitlement.

But if you ask for advice, you're showing interest in learning about them, their career, their network, their path and whatever they're knowledgeable about. And that's when the floodgates open. That's when people are willing to extend themselves the most. Not when you ask for a favor, but when you ask for advice. Advice doesn't require them to make a commitment outside of a quick phone call or coffee meeting, and people are always willing to give advice. Most people like to be helpful and giving advice also makes them feel good.

Another million-dollar secret is that you should never burn bridges with your connections because you never know when you will cross paths again. No matter how new you are to the work world or to your industry, I promise that this will happen, if it hasn't already.

Somebody you used to work with or someone in your network will pop back up on your radar. Maybe you're looking to switch jobs and this person works at a company you hope to work for. Or you might have to work with this person on some kind of project.

You get the picture. You never know when people from your past will resurface. It's imperative that you keep good relations with everyone.

Finally, keep in contact with your contacts. Ultimately, you want to make sure that you're always on their radar. You worked hard to get them in your network, so keep them there.

That doesn't mean you should email them every week, but don't become an afterthought in their minds. Drop them an email or call from time to time and let them know what you're up to and see how they are doing in return. This occasional contact will ensure that when a job becomes available or an opportunity arises that might benefit you, you're on their radar.

Get Social with Your Media

I can't even begin to explain the importance of social media in this day and age, especially when trying to network and advance your career. I could write books and books and books on this topic. But for our purposes, and in consideration of your time, I'll stick to a few paragraphs.

Look at it this way: If you're Charlie and you're trying to get into the Chocolate Factory, consider sites like LinkedIn and Facebook to be your golden tickets.

Most likely, you have an Instagram or TikTok account for posting pictures and music videos, commenting on friends' pictures, and posting status updates about the cool trip you're going on. What about the idea of your social media as relationship-building or networking tools to advance your career?

Most people get so caught up in the videos, pictures, likes, and comments that they forget there's vital information on social media. I'm not talking about info on what kind of car they bought or the new Jordans that just arrived at their house. I'm talking about information that could be your golden ticket in the career world! In addition to the cars and the Jordans (FWIW I do love a new pair of J's), social media can tell us who is friends with whom and the companies they work for, what cities they live in, and even the companies that are hiring.

Almost every day I see a post that says, "My Company is looking for a (insert job title here), send me your resume if you're interested." These are tremendous assets to your career-information arsenal. And best of all, this information is available right at your fingertips, and it is free and through your network where you likely have a connection.

See what we did there? We brought it full circle!

The ball is in your court now. So, get out there, get social, and get CONNECTED!

Chapter six

THE CHALLENGE

Networking is more about 'farming' than it is about 'hunting'. It's about cultivating relationships.

– Dr. Ivan Misner

Make your mark! All of your goals and connections begin with what you do with the information in this book, along with all of the nuggets that you learn along the way to help you foster your personal and professional growth. You've got your whole life to make your mark. However, the sooner you start, the longer you'll have to compound the positive results of making critical connections. When you're young, it can seem like you have plenty of time to master this stuff and you may not make it a priority. But let me just say how quickly you'll be looking back wondering where the time went, and you don't want to look back and regret missed opportunities to make connections. On the other hand, if you're already deep into your career, know that it's never too late.

Cultivating critical connections isn't just about the right now, it is also about where those connections have the possibility of taking you. I designed this challenge to help you think about what comes next in your career and how your connections can help take you there. The goal of the challenge is to keep you focused on cultivating critical connections even after you have stopped reading this book. What happens over the next weeks, months, and years is entirely up to you! If you put in the time and effort, you will be amazed at how your new connections can impact your success.

During this challenge you will have the opportunity to cultivate critical connections that will either put you at the top of your game or leave you starting from scratch. Imagining where you will be and what your goals will be in a few years from now can be daunting. You may be asking what is the best way to think five years ahead? The answer is to break it up into short-term and long-term goals that can help keep you on track.

Remember that cultivating critical connections is not about quantity; it is always about quality. It's not a sales transaction; it's always a service exchange. If you create your Connections Intention Vision Statement on those grounds, then you've already established your intent, and you're well on your way to success in making and maintaining critical connections.

Develop Your Critical 9

Building a network of thousands may work effectively for some, but again you run the risk of having loose, superficial connections. That is why I developed the idea of a Critical 9. Your Critical 9 are the core few connections that change the course of your life. These become the most vital connections to focus your attention on, especially when you are just starting out. But even when you have been cultivating critical connections for some time, your Critical 9 will be the core of your connecting efforts.

In the Connections chapter of this book, I talked about using the Connections Strategy Grid (CSG) to manage and track your critical connections. Today, technology has offered up many tools you can use to manage your connections. Choose the best platform for you. The CSG is a manual example of how to build your own tracking system. Take a look at that CSG list you filled out earlier. Consider the people on that list. Do any of them have life-changing potential? You may not meet your Critical 9 right away. In fact, it may take years, but each time you add someone to that list, keep in mind your goals and the criteria for your Critical 9.

Your Critical 9 are the nine people you will critically connect with during this challenge. These are the individuals who will impart wisdom, direction, and knowledge in your life, directly or indirectly, so you can grow professionally and personally. Sometimes someone you consider a Critical 9 doesn't directly contribute to your life on a regular basis. Instead, it could be that he or she made one significant contribution, at some point, which changed the trajectory of your life.

My first critical connection was the CEO of a Fortune 500 company. Looking back, I doubt he recognized how big an impact our connection had on me. Clearly the critical benefits of our relationship weighed heavier on my side, and it was up to me to keep the relationship intact. He was a CEO, I was a twenty-eight-year-old account manager, and we were far from a one-for-one match on what was mutually beneficial for us.

However, he took time out of his busy life to share his wisdom and support me when my confidence was at an all-time low, and he even went the extra mile of recommending me for future positions and allowed me to use him as a reference when opportunities arose. From that first essential connect, I developed my criteria for my Critical 9. I knew that the people who would become part of my Critical 9 would need the Level 5 leadership[6] qualities that I experienced with my first connection. Though it took many years to find the other eight, at least I knew what to look for and what would be the important features of a critical connection.

The criteria for your Critical 9 may be different from mine. You will have to determine what types of qualities you are looking for in those life-changing connections. Again, look at your CSG list. What are the qualities you gain the most benefits and insights from? Is it their position in a company? Is it the type of work they do? Or maybe it is how you connect with them.

My first critical connection was the first person I placed in what I call the Critical 9 Pyramid template. The lower five triangles that make up your pyramid form the foundation and will remain constant throughout your life. The upper four, however, may change over time as you, your skill level, and your goals grow and change. The things you gain and give to your connections will change, so some of those Critical 9 will have to change, too.

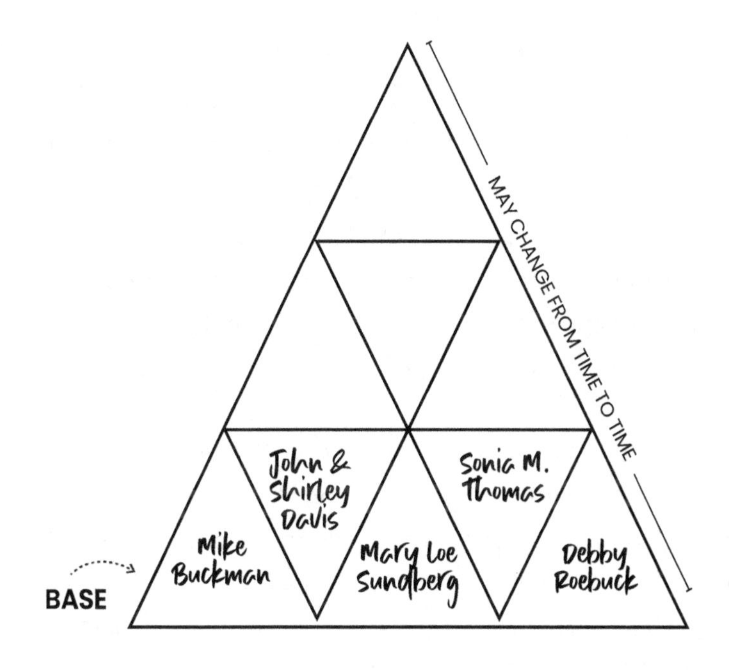

Find an Engaged Mentor

This may not come as new information to you, but it's worth repeating: Finding someone to mentor you during your years on this self-imposed challenge is of the utmost importance. Your current connections through friends, family, business associates, or fellow members of organizations in which you're active can help with your search to find the right mentor who can be your guide through this journey.

It's no easy feat finding a mentor who is willing to take on the responsibility required of a critical guide, but when you find someone with the mindset of giving back to those who are coming after him or her, you've hit the jackpot.

Make a list of all the potential mentors you, your family members or friends know. You'll want to consider what your specific career interests and goals are and who might be most helpful in those areas. Categorize each person by profession and start reaching out to each of them individually by calling them or sending an email. Don't be offended if some of your potential mentors say they don't have the time; this may happen quite often.

If you're just getting started in your career, you're in luck. You've got some time to get cracking. When you're just beginning, finding a mentor is much easier than trying to find one later. However, it's worth pursuing at any stage of your career. Once you've found your mentor, make sure you follow the Mindful Connector Method™ so you can assess whether the connection is mutually beneficial.

The Right College and Career Change Internships

I love Wikipedia's definition of an internship: "An internship is a system of on-the-job training. Although interns are typically college or university students, they can also be high school students or post-graduate adults. On occasion, they are middle school or even elementary students. Generally, the internship works as an exchange of services for experience between the student and his or her employer. They can also use an internship to determine if they have an interest in a career, create a network of contacts, or gain school credit. Some interns also find permanent, paid employment with the companies in which they interned. Thus, employers also benefit as experienced interns need little or no training when they begin full-time regular employment."

This definition of an internship is in perfect sync with our goals as critical connectors. An internship focuses on the mutual benefit of creating a learning opportunity for you while providing services for the business or professional you are interning for.

If you're still a student, then every spring, summer, and holiday break from college, you should be seeking out opportunities to intern. The benefit of internships is three-fold. First, internships provide a landscape of opportunities that will help you develop the necessary skills to be effective in your relationship building. Second, they allow you to figure out where you want to be and where your interests may lie. At this stage in your decision-making, you may not be completely clear on which jobs you're passionate about. That inner passion will become more apparent as you gain more experiences. Third, internships are a great opportunity and forum to practice the Mindful Connector Method™. So, the more internships you can garner for yourself, the better. Whenever possible, seek out jobs that align with your passion or are in the area you feel will most likely be your career choice.

I started interning in high school. Though interning during summers wasn't my first choice, it gave me the chance to make some money to help my mother out and I felt good about that. However, I also learned quite a bit about working with other people in a business environment, like how to speak up when necessary and how to make some valuable connections (people who remember me to this day). If I had this book then, those connections made during my high school years would surely have made it into my Critical 9.

Get Involved in Your Community

Get involved in your community because service is at the heart of everything worth doing, and it also gives you another platform for mastering the Mindful Connector Method™. There is important work to be done in your community: volunteering to feed the hungry, cleaning up the neighborhood park, working a fundraising event for a worthy cause. This work introduces you to a network of community leaders, elected officials, and philanthropists.

Find one or more local organizations to serve; it will do plenty for the heart and you may even find your career. Your goal is to make a commitment to get involved with your community at least once a month.

Start Now, Change Your Future

There are many ways you can choose to network and build relationships. How you cultivate critical connections, though, can change your life. I created the Mindful Connector Method™ described in this book so that I could help people who find cultivating critical connections challenging. For me, this comes easily and I'm grateful for that. But it does become easier when you practice the method and it becomes your own.

Though your journey in this area will change and evolve over the next few years, you will always grow professionally and personally when your intention to build critical connections is authentic from the beginning. Start now and change your future

Bonus Chapter #1

HOW TO RESPOND WHEN CONNECTIONS START GHOSTING

People may hear your words, but they feel your attitude.

– John C. Maxwell

I'm sharing my thoughts on ghosting in a way that will show grace and still promote growth. At least that's my intention. I'm still learning lessons from the ghosting phenomenon I've gotten from some of my most recent connections. It's amazing how it all happens and for no necessary reason. I will say with conviction that if you are getting ghosted by a connection you've made, you haven't made a "critical connection."

Let me give you the definition of the ghosting. Then I will share where and when it originated. Today it's moved from slang to officially being placed in Merriam-Webster's Dictionary. You can't get more official than that.

Ghosting is when you go poof and literally disappear out of someone's life without a word or explanation.[7]

The term ghosting had its relationship origins set in a parody to "Ghoster's Paradise" by Hannah VanderPoel, where she riffed about how we've all been there: You go on a few great dates with someone, things seem perfect, then you never hear from them again. It's an epidemic! This one is for you.[8]

Ghosting is mainly used in the language of the dating scene. How- ever, making professional connections is a lot like dating. You wouldn't think that ghosting would happen in these situations, but I've noticed that it's been happening more frequently in my circles. For example, you meet some-one at a networking event, you exchange business cards or have a really great conversation and you have an interest in that person's place of work or position. Sometimes the per-son you've connected with goes so far as to offer something to you or makes a promise to connect with you, and after you've followed up several times you never hear from them again. That's ghosting in a networking environment.

Let's explore this matter a little further. I have a couple of snackable ghosting stories I want to share.

Here's one such story of my friend and colleague Courtney, who took time to dig deeper into her ghosting urges. Her story helped me take a harder look at the other side of this dynamic called ghosting.

Courtney shares: As a woman, I've experienced an expec-tation to please others. I've noticed through exploration of some social conditioning that I've been taught and nurtured to put others' feelings above my own. Therefore, I found myself falling into patterns of unintentional ghosting. If I feel awkward with a potential connection I've made, it is far easier to just disappear than to articulate that moving forward with the connection is not something I want to pursue.

Investing time in my personal growth through reading and journaling, I've come to practice some language to avoid ghosting. It starts with taking responsibility for my thoughts and words, and just being honest. So, for instance, I may say something like:

- Thank you for considering me for this project, but I don't currently have the bandwidth to take this on. Perhaps I can recommend someone else?
- I'm honored you asked me to participate, however this doesn't align with my priorities/goals/mission. I wish you the best.
- I can't participate but I know your event will be a success. Thank you for the invitation.

On Being Ghosted

"It is easy to take it personally when I'm ghosted, but I can acknowledge the truth: It has nothing to do with me. Someone else's lack of ability shows me where they are; it is not a reflection of my value or worth. Looking back on my hesitation to say NO to a possible connection, I can have empathy. Additionally, because they have not communicated, I really don't know why they went missing. There can be several reasons why and to keep my peace of mind, I can assume the best and mind my own business until or if they contact me again," Courtney says.

Recently, I reached out to a female director of an innovative fin-tech company. My connection approach is always to ask straight out for a conversation via LinkedIn if I have an interest in a role or company, and apologize later, if I must. The response was immediate (well, when I say immediate, I mean within 48 hours). We set up a Zoom call for the same week and we had a great conversation about the role and the culture of the company and so many other anecdotal fillers—or so I thought. We ended our conversation with a few things to follow up on. 1) Me sending her a copy of my resume, 2) sending her a link to an older edition of this book, 3) she was going to talk to the recruiter that she knew personally, and 4) she was going to get me connected with a female entrepreneur friend of hers because she thought we had some synergies, etc. To me that was a win!

Well, I got GHOSTED with no explanation whatsoever! I emailed more than once, sent LinkedIn messages several times, and nothing.

What did happen was unexpected. I got an immediate email from the recruiter that said they weren't going to consider me for the role. The lesson here for me was I didn't need to know what happened. It didn't matter. As a critical connector, which is where I hope everyone reading this book is trying to evolve to, make sure your intentions and your words create the truth of who you are when you are connecting with people. This kind of scenario would never produce what I call a critical connection. This type of ghosting non-response is a deal breaker. I liken it to a lack of character.

The great thing about the Mindful Connector Method™ for cultivating critical connections is that you learn how to quickly determine whether additional pursuit of a connection is beneficial. The process helps you to develop and practice the steps for creating genuine relationships that are meaningful and mutually beneficial. So, don't waste your time and energy on connections that don't have the same thoughtfulness about the connections they make.

Bonus Chapter #2

THE NATURE OF CONNECTIONS WITH INFLUENCE

You can have everything in life you want if you will just help enough other people get what they want.

– Zig Ziglar

Some time ago an associate of mine mentioned that he had helped many people get jobs at various places over the years and for some reason, now, no one seemed to want to help him plug in and get work. I detected a hint of anger and resentment in my colleague's voice, so I wanted to dig deeper into what was really behind that energy, not only for him, but I also wondered if I was harboring some of the same stuff. Based on our conversation, I took time over a weekend to reflect on my own job search journey over the years and concluded, and wouldn't you know, I had some of that stuff, too. There is a significant difference between the connections you have with influence and those that don't have any. When you are looking to make a move from your current job or if you've been laid off from work, whatever your current state is, especially if you can't afford to be without work for too long, you've got to have connections with INFLUENCE.

Dictionary.com defines influence as, "The capacity or power of persons or things to be a compelling force on the actions, behavior, opinions, etc., of others." NOW THAT'S POWERFUL!

Connections with influence are those people who have the POWER to cause or prevent an action! I've seen it happen for me many times in years past. If you're not finding opportunities quickly, I will cautiously say that you don't have connections with influence, especially if you are an unconventional professional like me (i.e. diverse background, entrepreneurship, a little corporate, a little nonprofit, a little creative— you get it?). For the most part our work speaks for itself, and if you've done good work and your reputation precedes you, influential connections become our champions, making the job placement cycle shorter and with more impact.

We should never assume that the 500+ connections we may have will be able to have influential impact in our lives or when we are looking for jobs. INFLUENCE is earned. A person may have a title of director/VP/manager at a particular company or business and they may be a CONNECTION for you but it doesn't mean they can cause or prevent an action. Woo, this is good stuff. I'm encouraging myself. I'm building myself up.

Understanding these things in a job search journey will help you recalibrate and stop wasting time. I've learned that I must be more strategic in my approach to shortening that job placement cycle by connecting with people with influence, while cultivating and continuing to nurture the relationships with the people who don't have influence, in the event that one day, they will EARN it.

In this book I talk about creating a Connections Intention Vision Statement for how you will make connections for the rest of your life. Practicing this kind of strategic "setting the tone" for what you want your connections to look like and become in the long run will make your critical connecting, networking, net-weaving, whatever term you may use, easier and more dynamic. Let me be clear, obtaining and maintaining influential (critical) connections requires mutual work. It's not a one-sided arrangement, folks. Both parties in the connection relationship have to deem the connection critical enough to warrant the effort of keeping the connection intact. I'm not talking about the ACT of networking; I'm talking about the SPIRIT of it.

So, when you are out and about searching, connecting and asking for the job, don't be disturbed when your connections are unresponsive or distant. Put on a different hat and think about if you were in a position to cause someone to get a job or not; do you really have that influence? Your connections have good intentions; however, they may not have the influence to really make your job placement happen. Don't project your disappointment for not finding work on your connection (I'm speaking to myself here). Own the realization that there is more work to be done.

There has always been a method to how I have pursued making critical connections in my life. Sharing my process is personal. It is not rocket science, but it does stretch a person to go deeper into a space inside themselves that they may have never thought important to do, while establishing their professional networks. So, with these techniques in mind, I hope you go out there with a renewed mindset and the skills you need to transform your life, business, and career connections.

ACKNOWLEDGMENTS

Getting this book done was more than a notion, but not an afterthought.

I am grateful to Dr. Deborah Roebuck, who saw my potential as a contributor to the relationship-building community.

To Greg Goldner, the master connector, for his awesome contribution to this work and for always answering my calls.

To Dorothy, Jason, Richard, Elijah, and Kenneth. It was my personal experience with you and the C-Level executives you were paired with that inspired me to put pen to paper.

To all the other critical connections I have made over the years, thank you for allowing me into your life. I am who I am because of you.

ENDNOTES

[1] Hennigan, A. (2014-2017). Payforward Networking. (2nd ed.). (pp. 9-13). Amazon

[2] https://journals.sagepub.com/doi/full/10.1177/0001839214554990

[3] Cultivate. (n.d.). Retrieved from https://www.dictionary.com/browse/cultivate?s=t

[4] https://www.thebalancecareers.com/pareto-s-principle-the-80-20-rule-2275148

[5] https://www.dictionary.com/browse/code-switching

[6] https://www.jimcollins.com/concepts/level-five-leadership.html

[7] https://www.merriam-webster.com/dictionary/ghosting

[8] https://www.youtube.com/watch?v=X8oft8rQeaU
Directed by Michael Schwartz. Written by Hannah VanderPoel. Produced by Michael Schwartz and Hannah VanderPoel

ABOUT THE AUTHOR

Monique LaRue has a callaloo (Caribbean gumbo-style food) upbringing. Born in the Bronx, New York, and raised on the island of St. Croix, USVI, she spent her adolescence in Lakeland, Florida, and currently lives in Atlanta with her mother. She has an undergraduate degree from Morris Brown College (HBCU) and an MBA from Kennesaw State University.

Monique knew early on there was something unique about her ability to establish rapport quickly and with ease. Not fully understanding the significance or the inner working of that gift, Monique landed professional opportunities in the corporate arena and as a marketing and nonprofit consultant year after year.

As a professional black woman with that potential, she experienced some injustices at work and in business for moving up and forward—but she didn't quit. Her mother would often remind her that, "Baby, your gift will make room for you." (Proverbs 18:16). With that narrative from her mother playing out in her mind, she became a connected, creative, and entrepreneurial-minded leader.

Her social entrepreneurship game is fierce. And her passion for creating awareness for the underdog never ceases. She launched an adaptive apparel clothing line for people living with dementia, in honor of her mother; founded the National Black Customer Success Professionals group to level the playing field for black customer success professionals; and is the creator and publisher of a micro and small business magazine in support of nonprofit program initiatives.

ABOUT GREG GOLDNER

Greg Goldner was born and raised in Atlanta, Georgia, and currently lives in Arizona. As a graduate of the University of Arizona, Greg knew from a young age that he was born with the gift of gab. He thanks his grandmother Naomi for that. From early on, Greg has used his ability to talk to anyone to network himself into a role as a national television news and entertainment correspondent and to ultimately solidify himself as a master connector.

He's a 2x Emmy Award winner with 15 years of experience at the intersection of marketing, media and brands. He is a unique hybrid of marketing executive and creative director who leads by example and thrives on moving the needle with engaging marketing initiatives. His entrepreneurial hustle and solution-oriented mentality allows him to bring a sense of calmness during times of chaos.